READING

Adventures
by Land, Air, and Water

Program Authors

Connie Juel, Ph.D.

Jeanne R. Paratore, Ed.D.

Deborah Simmons, Ph.D.

Sharon Vaughn, Ph.D.

PEARSON

Scott
Foresman

Glenview, Illinois
Boston, Massachusetts
Chandler, Arizona
Upper Saddle River, New Jersey

ISBN-13: 978-0-328-45290-3
ISBN-10:   0-328-45290-4

7 8 9 10 V011 14 13

CC1

UNIT 5   Contents

Adventures
by Land, Air, and Water

What can we do in emergencies?

What surprises can the past hold for us?

ADVENTURES AND HEROES 57

How can adventures change us?

EXTREME HOMES 83

What do people give up to live in certain places?

THE MOON 109

Why does the moon fascinate us?

EMERGENCIES

Contents

Words 2 the Wise

It's an emergency!
What do you do?
Who can help?
Read to find out how
you can prepare for
emergencies.

Let's Explore

QUICK THINKING

Call 9-1-1 to get help during an emergency.

The nine-year-old boy didn't know what to do. His mom was choking on a piece of candy. She couldn't breathe. Then he remembered something. Call 9-1-1! The dispatcher* told him how to do the Heimlich maneuver (HIME-lick muh-NOO-vuhr). He squeezed his mom below the ribs, and the candy popped out. The boy's quick thinking saved his mother's life. He was a hero!

dispatcher* person who answers 9-1-1 calls

An emergency is a dangerous or serious situation. It must be handled quickly. Police officers, firefighters, and paramedics all respond to emergencies. They help people who need medical attention. This could be someone who is injured, choking, or not breathing. Rescue workers also respond when there is a fire or when someone is committing a crime.

Rescue workers respond quickly in an emergency.

What should you do in an emergency? First, tell an adult or call 9-1-1. If you do call 9-1-1, a dispatcher will ask you a series of questions. Listen carefully. Answer the questions. Stay on the phone. The dispatcher will send someone to help or tell you what to do.

Emergencies can be scary, but you can take steps to prepare for them. An emergency checklist can help.

ENTERING:

911

Options   Main Menu

Practice what to say during a 9-1-1 call.

Emergency Phone Numbers

Emergency: 9-1-1

Mom's cell: 555-1234

Dad's cell: 555-1235

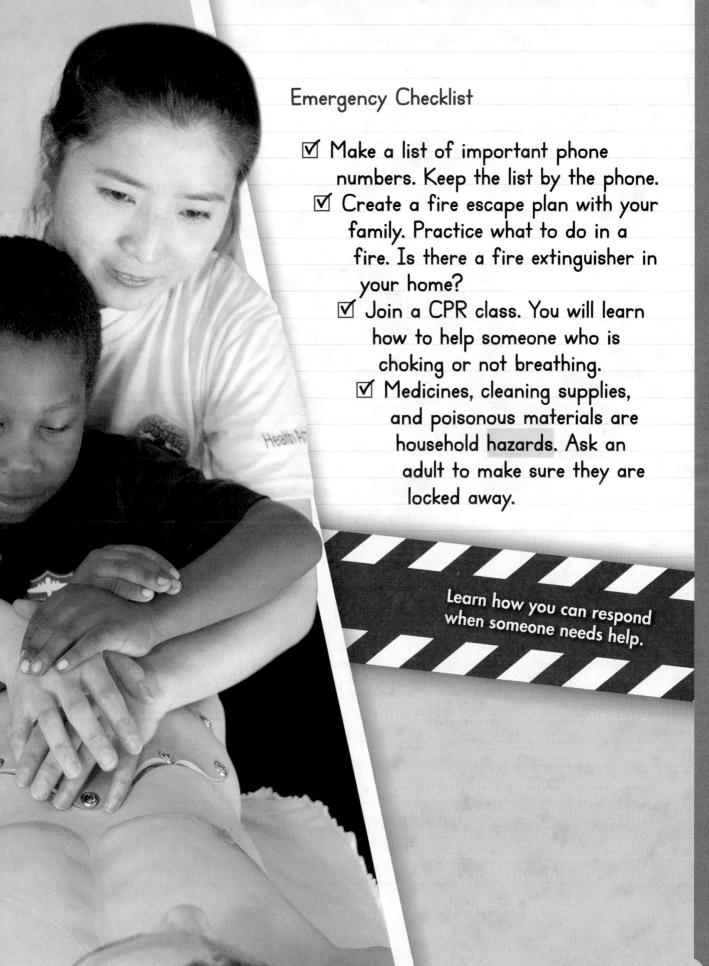

Emergency Checklist

- ☑ Make a list of important phone numbers. Keep the list by the phone.
- ☑ Create a fire escape plan with your family. Practice what to do in a fire. Is there a fire extinguisher in your home?
- ☑ Join a CPR class. You will learn how to help someone who is choking or not breathing.
- ☑ Medicines, cleaning supplies, and poisonous materials are household hazards. Ask an adult to make sure they are locked away.

Learn how you can respond when someone needs help.

Heroes Who

Rescue workers respond to all types of emergencies.

A 9-1-1 call comes in. Who will respond? Paramedics, firefighters, and lifeguards are all heroes who help in an emergency. Their work is exciting, but it can be dangerous too.

Paramedics

Paramedics respond to many types of emergencies. They may treat a person injured in a fall, a car crash, a flood, or an earthquake. Paramedics must quickly size up a problem. Then they decide what kind of care is needed. Their goal is to get patients to the hospital as quickly and as safely as possible.

Help

by Karen Sandoval

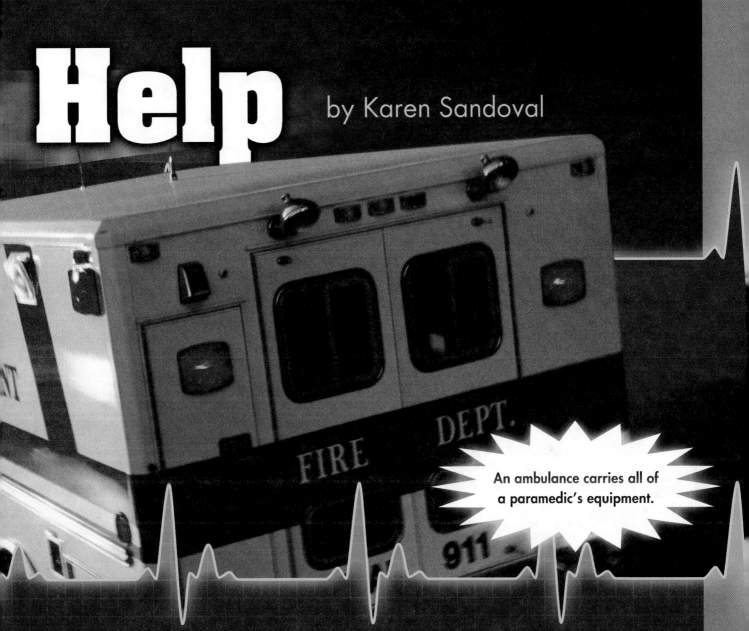

An ambulance carries all of a paramedic's equipment.

Paramedics must complete more than one thousand hours of training. They learn how to treat cuts, burns, and broken bones. They also learn how to treat more severe injuries.

A paramedic's most visible tool is an ambulance. This vehicle holds all the equipment paramedics need. They use bandages, cold packs, and splints. In more severe cases, they may use breathing masks or a heart monitor.

Firefighters

It's a fire! Firefighters are the heroes who respond to this emergency. They save people trapped in burning buildings. But not all calls involve fires. Firefighters also rescue people after disasters. They even clean up destroyed buildings.

Like paramedics, firefighters spend many hours in training. They learn how fire spreads. This knowledge helps them decide the best way to put out a fire and how to avoid dangerous areas. Firefighters also have medical training.

A firefighter's job can be dangerous.

Firefighters' clothing helps protect them from the hazards of their profession. Heavy coats shield them from intense heat. Helmets protect them from falling objects. Masks and air packs help them breathe.

Firefighters use various tools. With the Jaws of Life, they free people trapped in cars. If paramedics have not yet arrived, firefighters use medical supplies to treat accident victims.

Firefighters wear special clothing for protection.

15

Lifeguards

Lifeguards work in or near the water. Unlike other rescue workers, they work right where an emergency might happen.

Lifeguards protect swimmers at pools, beaches, and water parks. Beach lifeguards watch for signs that point to dangerous swimming conditions. They may have to rescue a swimmer who cannot get back to shore. Pool lifeguards enforce safety rules.

Lifeguards are always on the lookout for any emergency.

spine board

Lifeguards must be strong swimmers. In training, they learn how to rescue a drowning person. They must be able to carry victims to safety. Lifeguards also receive some medical training. They may have to treat victims who are not breathing.

Like other rescue workers, lifeguards use special equipment. Sometimes, swimmers have spinal injuries. Lifeguards use a spine board to move these victims. Rescue tubes and rescue cans are other tools that lifeguards might use to pull swimmers to safety.

rescue can

rescue tube

GUARD

17

Other Duties

Rescue workers are heroes every day. They help us even when there is not an emergency. Paramedics teach first-aid classes. Firefighters present fire safety programs. Lifeguards teach swimming classes. The men and women in these professions all work hard to prevent emergencies.

Rescue workers also help prevent emergencies.

You Can Help

Emergencies can happen at any time, in any place. What can you do? If someone needs help, tell an adult or call 9-1-1. Learn what to do if someone is choking. Learn how to give first aid. Collect food and clothing for disaster victims. Or help raise money for a special fund. You too can be a hero who helps.

Collecting food is one way to be a hero who helps.

What Do You Think?

How are the rescue workers you read about alike? How are they different?

CALLING NEW SMOKEJUMPERS

by Anne Beier
illustrated by Neil Shigley

Steve felt nervous. For the first time his uncle was going to leave him alone in the smokejumpers' cabin.

"Call me on the walkie-talkie if there's trouble," Uncle Henry said. "Don't worry. You've learned a lot this summer."

Uncle Henry chose to be a smokejumper as his profession. Now, Steve wasn't so sure that he could be one too. Smokejumpers had to parachute into areas where there were fires.

Steve was excited about spending his summer vacation in Montana. His uncle had a dangerous but exciting job. Steve told his parents that he wanted to be a smokejumper too. So they agreed to let him spend the summer with his uncle.

Suddenly the phone rang. A red emergency light flashed on the phone. Steve grabbed the walkie-talkie. "Uncle Henry, can you read me?" Steve asked. "There's an emergency call. Please return to base!"

Then Steve answered the emergency call. "Montana Smokejumper Base. This is Steve."

"This is the 9-1-1 operator," the voice said. "I'm connecting you to Steve at the smokejumper base. Tell him your name, and describe your situation."

"My name is Jim Park," another voice said excitedly. "A storm just came through the area. Lightning started a fire! There's a lot of smoke in the distance. It's moving towards our house at the PK Ranch!"

"Where are you now?" Steve asked.

"I'm in the house with my dog. My parents are out running errands."

Uncle Henry hurried through the door. Steve handed him the receiver.

"Son, we need you to sit tight," Uncle Henry said. "I want you to stay on the phone with Steve until we get there."

"Okay," Jim replied. "But please hurry!"

Uncle Henry handed the receiver back to Steve. "Try to keep him calm and have the walkie-talkie on too," Uncle Henry said.

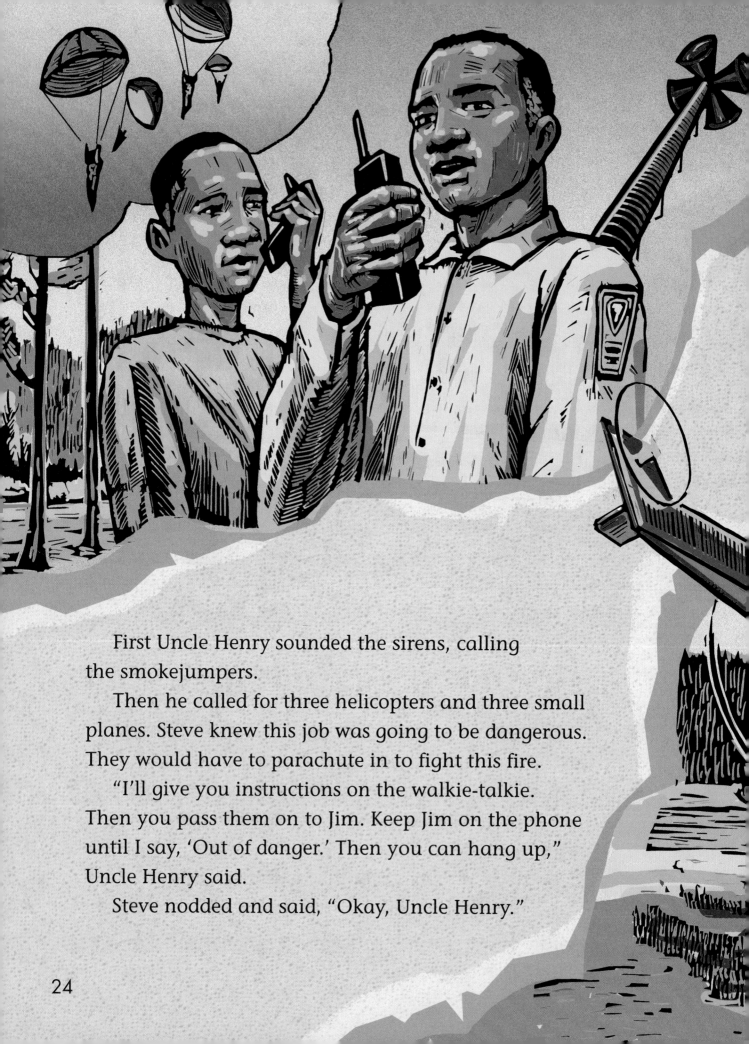

First Uncle Henry sounded the sirens, calling the smokejumpers.

Then he called for three helicopters and three small planes. Steve knew this job was going to be dangerous. They would have to parachute in to fight this fire.

"I'll give you instructions on the walkie-talkie. Then you pass them on to Jim. Keep Jim on the phone until I say, 'Out of danger.' Then you can hang up," Uncle Henry said.

Steve nodded and said, "Okay, Uncle Henry."

Steve began talking to Jim. "Jim, the smokejumpers will be there soon. Are you okay?"

"So far. Do you live in Montana, Steve?" Jim asked.

"No, I'm from New York. I'm working with my uncle for the summer. I wanted to see what it is like to be a smokejumper."

"Have you jumped from any planes?"

"No, not yet," Steve answered. "Mostly I clean the trails. And I make sure the smokejumpers have their first-aid supplies and food."

"That sounds like fun," Jim said.

"I like watching the smokejumpers parachute into areas to put out fires."

"The wall of fire is getting closer," Jim shouted. "Wait! I hear a helicopter over my house."

"Steve!" Uncle Henry said over the walkie-talkie. "Tell Jim to go outside!"

"Can you get outside?" Steve asked.

"I can climb on the roof," he answered.

"Do that now! A smokejumper will come down on a cable. They'll pull you and the dog up to the helicopter. Go!"

Steve could hear the helicopter. Finally, he heard Uncle Henry through the walkie-talkie, "Out of danger, Steve."

Steve smiled and then hung up the phone.

The next day was exciting too. Everyone congratulated Steve on how well he did. Best of all, he was more sure than ever about what he wanted to be someday. He had decided on his profession—a smokejumper!

WHAT DO YOU THINK?

How does Steve feel about being a smokejumper at the beginning of the story? How does he feel about it at the end?

Satellite photos can show smoke from wildfires.

Wild

Orange powder keeps the fire from spreading.

What can start a wildfire? It could be lightning or a campground fire left burning.

A fire needs fuel, air, and heat to burn. Fuel is present in grasses, twigs, and trees. Air is all around. Heat comes from hot, dry weather. Firefighters try to fight these three powerful elements.

On the ground, firefighters start new fires to cut off the fuel. If the wind blows in the right direction, this might work.

fires!

Firefighters drop water from helicopters or airplanes. This controls the heat. They also drop a soupy mixture called slurry. This helps cut off the fire's air supply. Fighting fires is dangerous and not always successful.

How can people keep the fires from starting? NASA* is helping to prevent wildfires. Satellite photos can show the danger zones. Then firefighters can go to the spot and attack the danger before a wildfire spreads.

* National Aeronautics and Space Administration

4 you 2 Do

Word Play

Use any of the letters in the words below to make new words about emergencies. You can reread the stories for hints.

hero   exciting
dangerous   hazards
destroyed   profession

Making Connections

Do you think Steve would make a good firefighter? a good paramedic? a good lifeguard? Choose one profession and tell why you think Steve would be good at it.

On Paper

Write a fire escape plan to share with your family.

Possible answers for Word Play: aid, dispatcher, escape,
fire, hurt, protect, rescue, respond, safety

PAST Times

Contents

Past Times

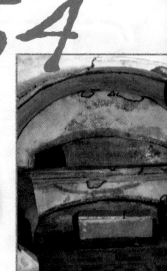

Words 2 the Wise

The past is all around us. Where do you see the past in your daily life? As you read, think about how learning about **past times** might help us better understand the present.

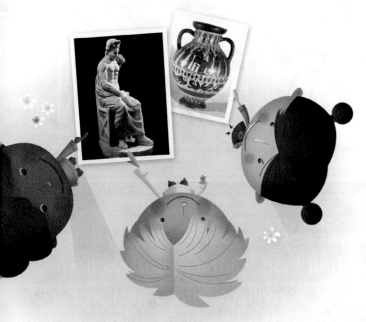

33

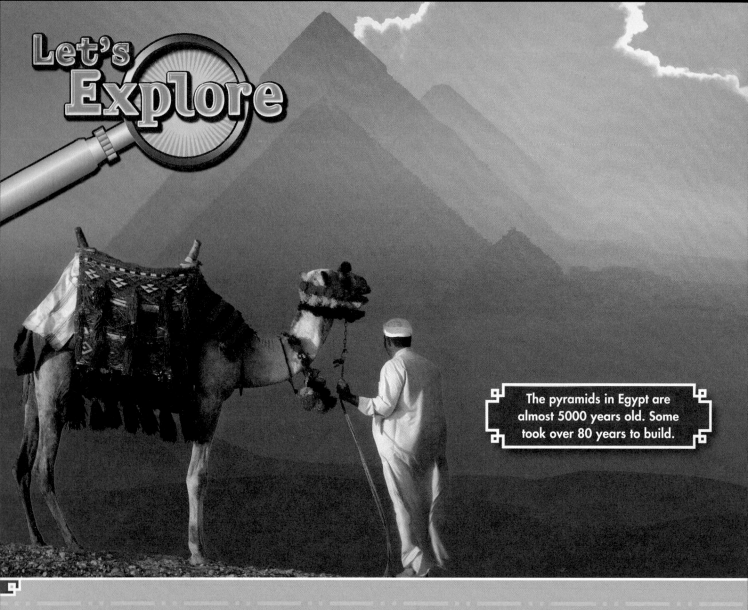

The pyramids in Egypt are almost 5000 years old. Some took over 80 years to build.

CIVILIZATION

Long ago, people found that it was easier to survive if they worked together. This helped them find food, clothing, and shelter. About 3,500 B.C. civilization began. A civilization is a group of people who work together in many ways. They build cities. They create laws. They make art.

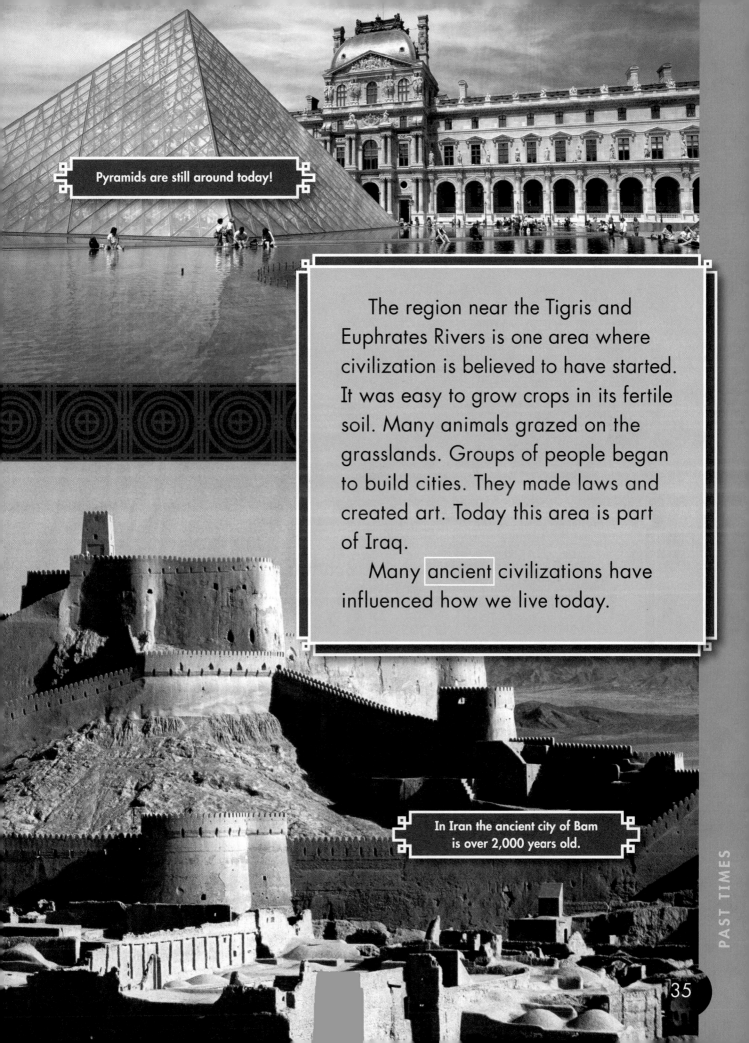

Pyramids are still around today!

The region near the Tigris and Euphrates Rivers is one area where civilization is believed to have started. It was easy to grow crops in its fertile soil. Many animals grazed on the grasslands. Groups of people began to build cities. They made laws and created art. Today this area is part of Iraq.

Many ancient civilizations have influenced how we live today.

In Iran the ancient city of Bam is over 2,000 years old.

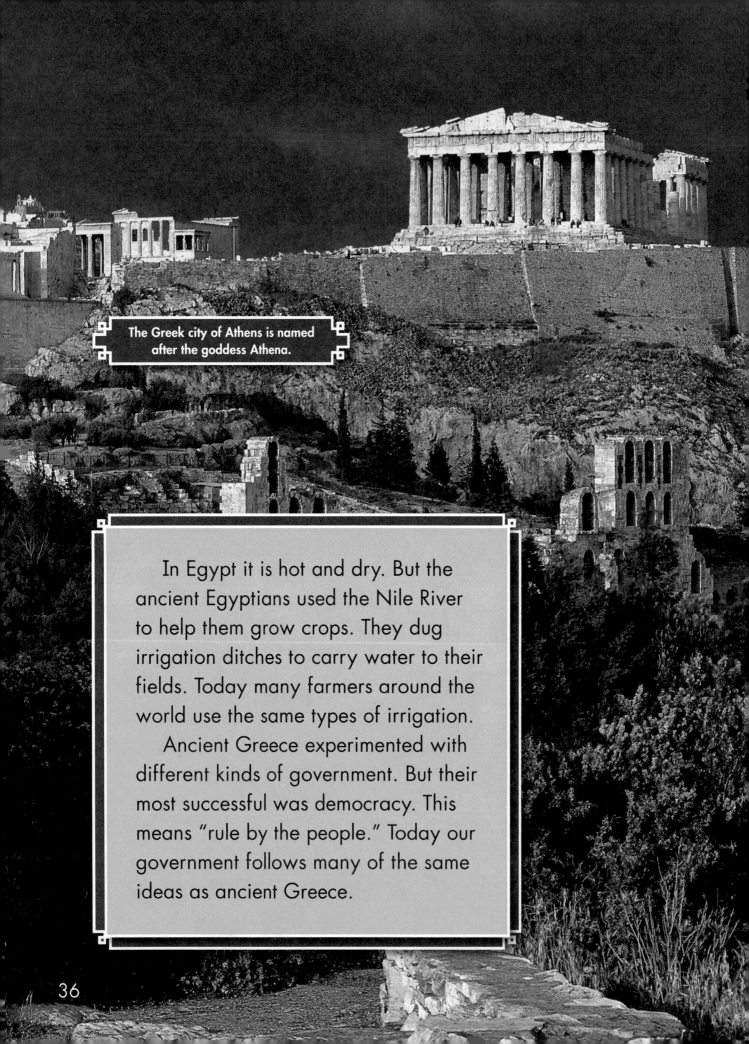

The Greek city of Athens is named after the goddess Athena.

In Egypt it is hot and dry. But the ancient Egyptians used the Nile River to help them grow crops. They dug irrigation ditches to carry water to their fields. Today many farmers around the world use the same types of irrigation.

Ancient Greece experimented with different kinds of government. But their most successful was democracy. This means "rule by the people." Today our government follows many of the same ideas as ancient Greece.

Iroquois leaders were chosen by women.

Native Americans also influenced our government. The Iroquois (IHR-uh-kwoy) lived in Canada and the northeastern United States. Early settlers found that their peaceful government was very organized. It is believed that the writers of our Constitution were influenced by the Iroquois system of government.

Our buildings, our government, and our art have all been influenced by past times. What do you think our civilization will pass on to the future?

Many buildings in the United States copy the same style as Greek buildings.

ANCIENT

by Tim Prentiss

Many Native American groups were named because of their beliefs or what they left behind. One of these groups was the Mound People. Their civilization settled along the Mississippi and Ohio Rivers. They also lived along Lake Erie and the Gulf of Mexico.

There were several different groups of Mound People. Each group formed its own society. Each group spoke a different language and had different traditions. Each group hunted and gathered food in different ways.

BUILDERS

This serpent mound is almost a quarter of a mile long.

But the Mound People had one thing in common. They all built mounds made from earth. Some were tall. Some were shaped like animals. Some were small mountains in the middle of flat land. Underneath lay the history of their civilization.

Many of the mounds covered the tombs of their greatest leaders. These tombs were large graves. It was where their leaders were buried with their things. It was a way to honor the leaders of the Mound People.

This mound was once part of the ancient city of Cahokia in A.D. 700

Mound People built large buildings in a central location. They used wood and mud as materials. Often the leader would live there. The building became his tomb when he died. Then the people would build a mound over the tomb.

The building of a new mound was a great celebration. Everyone helped pile bucket after bucket of dirt in one place. On top of this mound, the people would build a new building.

BUILDING A NEW MOUND WAS A GREAT CELEBRATION.

Many mounds were destroyed by farmers because they didn't know what they were.

The new leader would live in this building. One day a mound would also be built over that leader's building. Over time, the mounds grew higher. The Cahokia (ka-HOE-ki-a) mound in Illinois was 100 feet tall. Some were no higher than three feet. In the northern Great Lakes, mounds were often low. They were built in shapes such as birds, reptiles, and other animals. How did the Mound People know how to design these? They were skilled architects.

MOUND PEOPLE LEFT

BEHIND JEWELRY,

KNIVES, AND POTTERY.

In the 1700s, American settlers discovered
many of these mounds while hunting for food. They
found many mounds the size of small hills. Some of
these mounds were later plowed down for farming.
At the time, the settlers did not know the importance
of these places.

They did not think of the mounds as burial
places. They did not treat these areas and artifacts
with respect.

These mounds in Ohio had a golf course built over them.

In 1770, Joseph Tomlinson discovered a mound in West Virginia. He was curious about it, but he did not think it was worth preserving or protecting. The mound was dug up.

A relative of Joseph Tomlinson later opened a museum in the center room of the mound. He charged 25 cents to see the inside of the mound. Then in the 1860s, soldiers mounted cannons on it to fight during the Civil War.

The Aztec pyramids (left) were similar to mounds found in the United States (right).

One of the oldest mounds was found in West Virginia. It was built around 250 B.C. The Mound People buried their dead with jewelry and other artifacts. It is interesting that many other civilizations around the world had this same tradition.

Some mounds were similar to ancient Aztec pyramids in Central America. They had four sloped sides. The top was flat. Dirt was dug out from around the mound. Sometimes a ditch, or even a moat, was created.

The architecture of the Mound People is part of American history. The grassy mounds are a lasting mark of their civilizations. Today many states have preserved these ancient places. This helps future generations learn about the past.

WHAT DO YOU THINK?

How were the mounds different from each other?

It's Still Standing!

by Carol Pugliano-Martin
illustrated by Chris Lensch

Chris was showing Katie and Alex pictures from his vacation in Greece.

"What's that?" Katie asked, staring at a building with long white columns.

"It's a temple dedicated to the gods called the Parthenon (PAHR-thuh-nahn)," Chris replied. "The ancient Greeks held religious ceremonies there."

"That's cool," Alex said.

"It's almost 2,500 years old," said Chris. "And it's still standing!"

46

"Wow!" Katie said. "I've never seen anything that old before."

Alex picked up a picture of a theater with rows of stone seats. The seats all faced an open area in the shape of a circle. "What's this?" he asked.

"That is the theater at Delphi (DEL-fy)," Chris answered. "It's almost 2,500 years old too."

"More than 5,000 people could watch plays and listen to music there," Chris said.

47

Katie picked up a picture of a statue. A man was sitting on a throne. "Who's this?"

"Oh, that's a statue of Zeus, king of the Greek gods."

"Is that made of marble?" Alex asked.

"Yes," Chris said. "And that's an amphora (AM-for-ah), Katie."

Katie was holding a picture of a clay vase that had two handles.

"That was a jug used for carrying oil and other things. This artifact was discovered on a ship that was 2,300 years old!" Chris explained.

"This town seems so boring compared to Greece," said Katie.

"Well, boring or not, we have a soccer game tomorrow. Are we going to the park to practice or not?" Alex asked.

"Let's go," said Chris.

The three friends left Chris's house and started walking to the park. The bells of the town hall rang as they walked past. They gonged twice.

"Two o'clock," Katie said. "I never need to wear a watch with those bells."

"My great-great-great-grandfather helped build the town hall," Katie continued.

"Hey, look at this sign. I never noticed it before," said Alex. "It says 'A.D. 1845.' That's pretty old."

"In another 2,000 years it will be almost as old as the Parthenon," Katie said.

"Do you think it will still be here?" asked Chris.

"I'm sure it will," said Katie.

"Well let's go. If we stand here any longer, the bells will be ringing again," said Chris.

The friends reached the park. A red bird flew low towards them. It landed on a statue in front of the town hall.

"Look, a cardinal!" shouted Alex.

The bird flew away.

"Nice going, Alex!" groaned Katie.

"Should we call you the bird-man?" joked Chris.

"Speaking of man, who's this?" asked Alex. He examined the statue that the bird had landed on.

"Oh, him?" said Chris. "That's John Henry Preston. He was mayor of this town for a long time."

"That statue has been here for a long time," said Katie. "How did you miss it?"

"Too busy bird-watching," laughed Chris.

"Hey, maybe old Mr. Preston will still be standing here in 2,000 years," said Alex.

"Maybe," said Chris. "But he is no Greek god."

"No, but being mayor of a town for so long is pretty cool," said Katie.

"Hey, Chris," said Alex. "Remember when your dad and his old band played at the band shell here?"

"Yeah. The outdoor concerts were great. The park was packed. This band shell reminds me of the theater at Delphi," said Chris.

"You know, maybe this town isn't so boring after all," said Chris. "Hey, who did this?" he said as he picked up an empty soda can.

"Maybe someday it will be an ancient artifact," joked Alex.

"Yes," laughed Katie.

"Well, I think I'll just put this ancient artifact in the recycling bin!" laughed Chris.

What Do You Think?
How are the places in Chris's town similar to those in Greece?

Forever Sleeping Under Rome

One of the most popular tourist attractions in Italy is a burial place. It's the Roman catacombs (KAT-uh-komz).

The catacombs are a web of underground tunnels. Ancient Romans carved out spaces in tunnels to bury their families. The law in Rome stated that the dead must be buried with respect. In ancient Rome, burying people in the catacombs was a way to honor them.

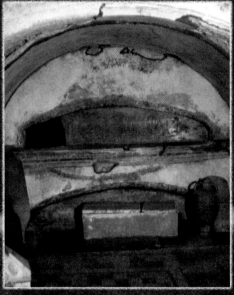

This is a catacomb in Rome.

Bodies were placed on small shelves inside the catacombs. Richer families bought larger spaces. That way they could be buried near each other.

People sometimes left vases or other artifacts to decorate the tombs. They also painted art on the walls. Over time, Romans began burying their dead in cemeteries. The catacombs were soon forgotten.

But centuries later, the catacombs were discovered again. Now people feel they are uncovering the history of "underground Rome."

55

4 YOU 2 DO

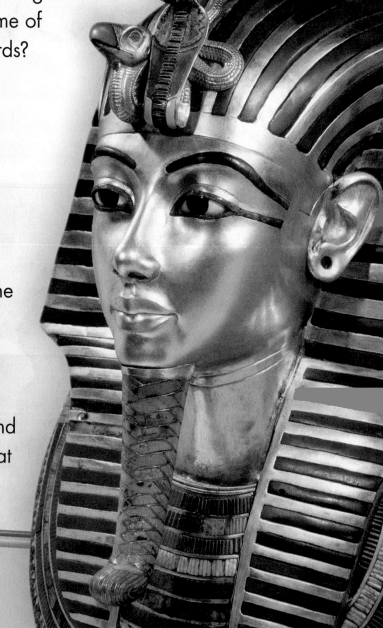

Word Play

Imagine that you were digging in your backyard, and you found pieces of letters scattered in an old wooden box. Can you rearrange these letters to discover some of this week's vocabulary words?

tiviclinzaio
tanniec
stradoitin

Making Connections

How are the mounds like the statue of Mayor Preston?

On Paper

Imagine that you have found an ancient artifact. Tell what it is and how it was used.

Answers for Word Play: civilization, ancient, traditions

ADVENTURES AND HEROES

Contents

ADVENTURES AND HEROES

Let's Explore

58

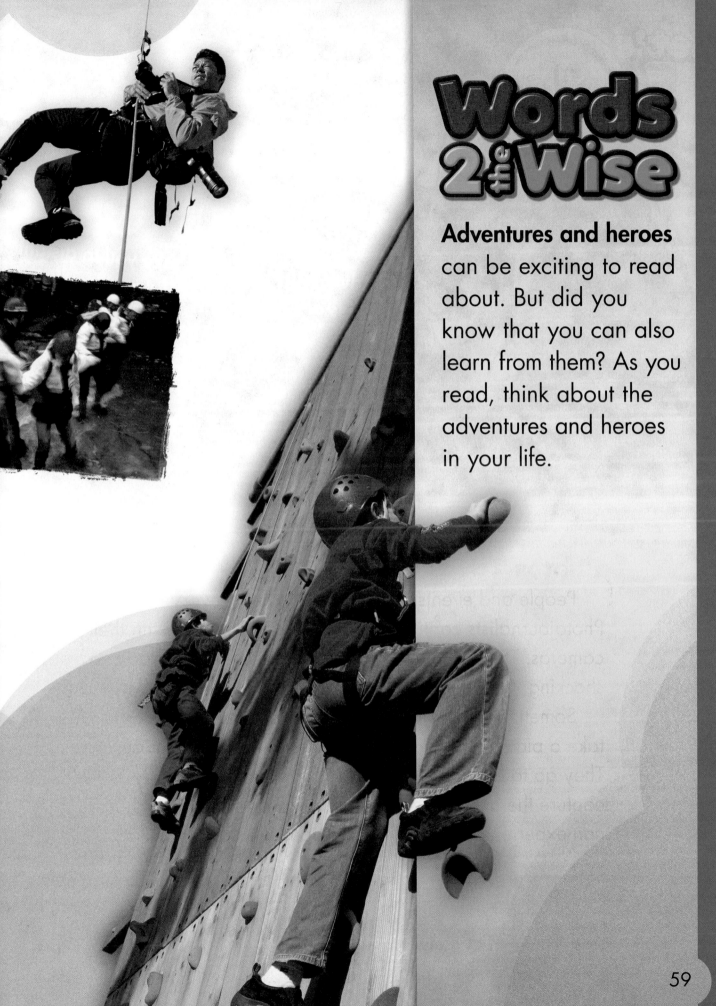

Words 2 the Wise

Adventures and heroes can be exciting to read about. But did you know that you can also learn from them? As you read, think about the adventures and heroes in your life.

59

Adventure on the

Adventurous jobs can take you to distant cities or to the bottom of the ocean.

Photos Tell the Story

People and events are making the news every day. Photojournalists capture these people and events with their cameras. Their photographs tell stories. Some are tragic or shocking. Others are joyful.

Sometimes photojournalists go to dangerous places to take a picture. They climb mountains in the wilderness. They go to disaster areas. They have to move quickly to capture the action. Because of their work, people at home can experience what is happening in distant places.

Job

Chasing Storms

Most people run for shelter in a storm, but storm chasers drive many miles to find storms! They often go to unfamiliar places looking for tornadoes.

Chasers are not foolish people. Many are scientists or teachers. They listen to weather forecasts and watch the skies. They want to learn how these amazing storms happen.

But chasers have to be careful. Heavy rain and fierce winds can flood the roads and blow down trees.

Underwater Frontier

Oceanographers study the ocean. They work at sea in a floating lab. They track ocean currents and underwater volcanoes. They study plant and animal life deep in the sea.

Sometimes these scientists travel deep underwater in submarines. After these expeditions, they use computers to make maps of the ocean floor.

Oceanographers must watch weather conditions at all times. They look for dangerous storms that can produce water surges. They must be prepared for extreme weather.

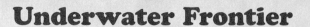

The Scene of a Crime

Crime scene investigators help solve mysteries. They use their toolboxes to collect clues. They gather evidence, such as hair, fabric, or fingerprints. They put all the facts together to solve mysteries.

Investigators at a crime scene watch for hidden dangers. They check for chemicals and weapons. Sometimes they wear protective gear and clothing.

Can you hear the call to adventure? The world is filled with adventurous jobs!

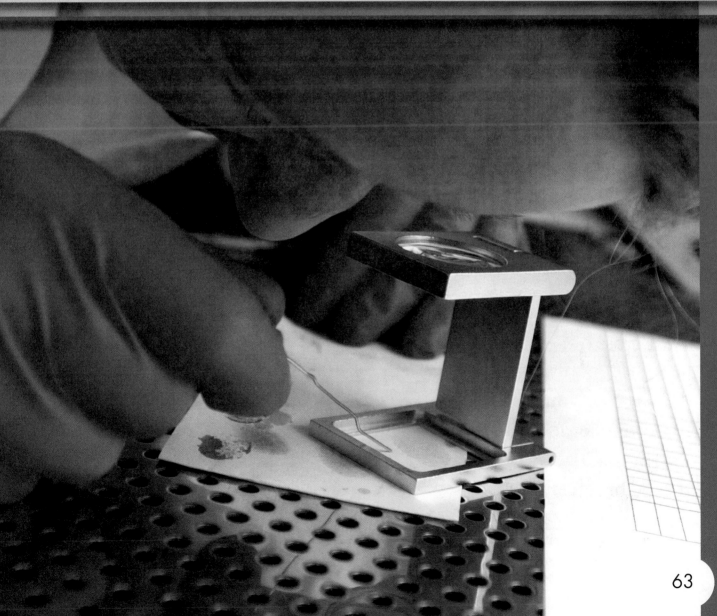

A LESSON IN
ADVENTURE

by Charlotte Clark

Today, your student team must cross a river. However, you have to find a way to get across the river without getting your backpacks or food wet.

The solution is to build a rope bridge. First you take one piece of rope and tie it around the trunk of a tree that is along the river. Then you tie another piece of rope around the same tree but about four feet higher. Now comes the hard part.

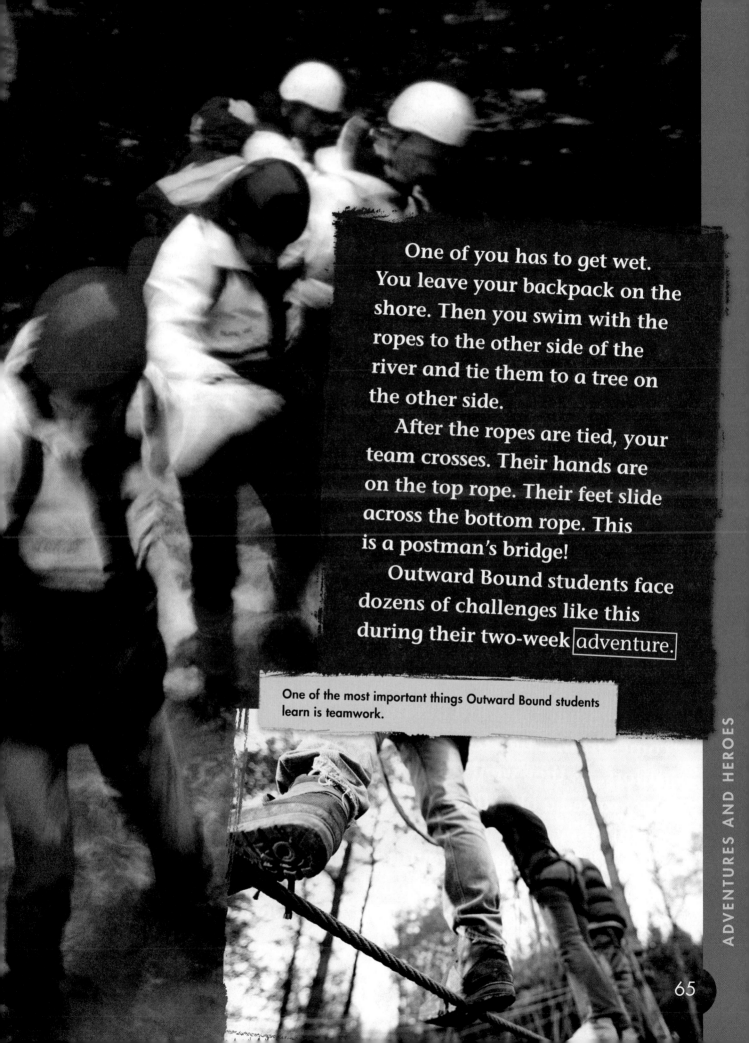

One of you has to get wet. You leave your backpack on the shore. Then you swim with the ropes to the other side of the river and tie them to a tree on the other side.

After the ropes are tied, your team crosses. Their hands are on the top rope. Their feet slide across the bottom rope. This is a postman's bridge!

Outward Bound students face dozens of challenges like this during their two-week adventure.

One of the most important things Outward Bound students learn is teamwork.

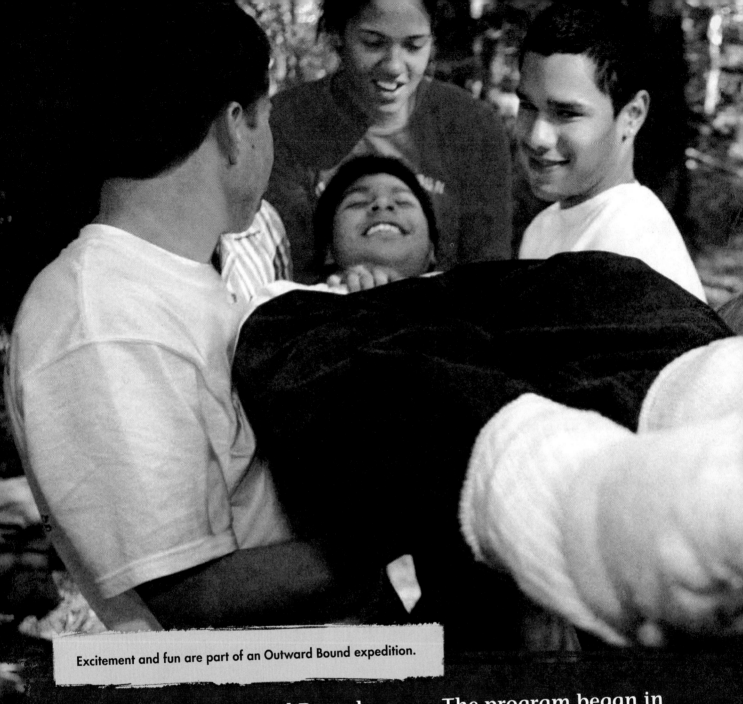

Excitement and fun are part of an Outward Bound expedition.

The name Outward Bound comes from a flag used by sailors. As they went to sea, they raised a blue flag. This meant they were "outward bound." They knew adventure lay ahead on their expeditions. Outward Bound students enjoy similar experiences.

The program began in England during World War II. The first Outward Bound program in the United States started in Colorado in 1962. Now there are many programs for both boys and girls around the world.

Outward Bound teaches students to face the challenges of the wilderness. During these adventures they learn how to survive and respect nature.

"Leave No Trace" is one goal of Outward Bound. This means they keep their campgrounds clean. They don't leave garbage. They make sure that all fires are out.

But the courses are not just about wilderness survival. They also teach students important lessons that they will remember for the rest of their lives.

Outward Bound teams rely on collaboration to be sure everyone is healthy and safe.

Do you have what it takes to survive in the wilderness? This is what many students discover about themselves. Your body and your mind have to be strong.

Students also learn how to lead and how to help one another. No student can climb a rock wall alone. But as a team, they can all reach the top safely.

In the evening, Outward Bound students are asked to write about their daily expeditions. This helps them learn about themselves.

Student adventures are on both land and water.

68

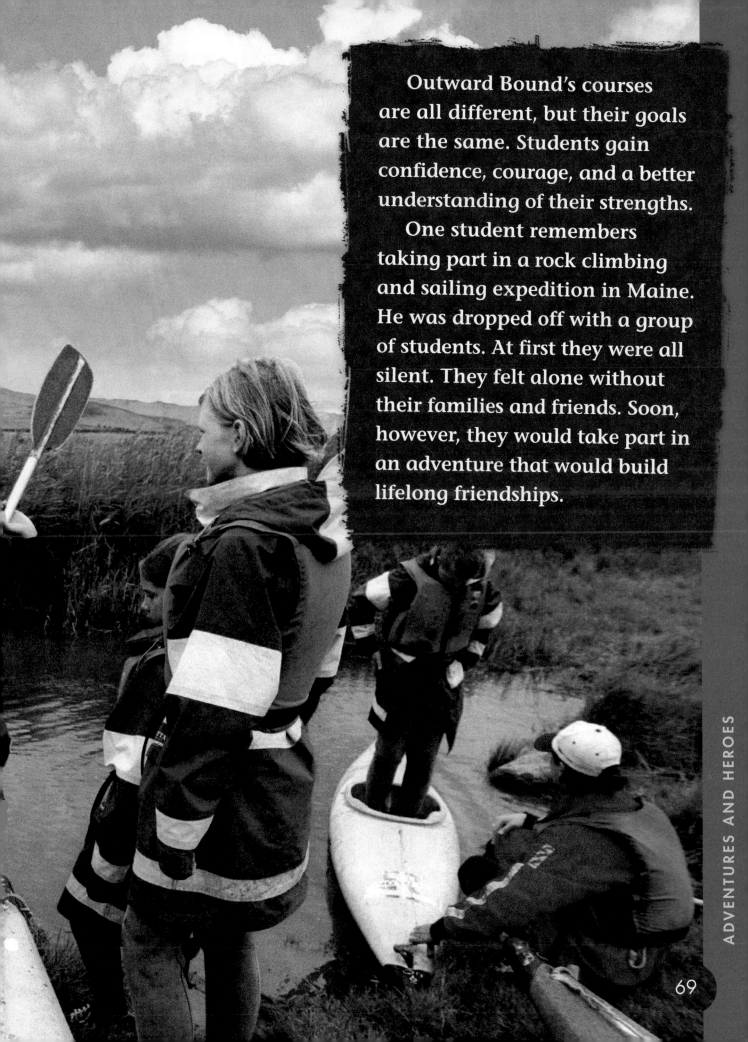

Outward Bound's courses are all different, but their goals are the same. Students gain confidence, courage, and a better understanding of their strengths.

One student remembers taking part in a rock climbing and sailing expedition in Maine. He was dropped off with a group of students. At first they were all silent. They felt alone without their families and friends. Soon, however, they would take part in an adventure that would build lifelong friendships.

Could you spend a week on a sailboat?

The students lived on a 30-foot boat. They learned to sail along the coast of Maine. When there was not much wind, they rowed.

They slept on the boat. At night, they covered themselves to protect against rain and mosquitoes.

After one week, they sailed to an island. There they spent four days. They learned to live in the wilderness and rock climb. For many students, it was the best experience of their lives.

Outward Bound programs are available across the United States. You can enjoy rafting, hiking, boating, and many other activities. Along the way, you will meet these challenges with confidence. You will work with a team to reach a common goal. You will help make sure that you and your teammates are always safe.

Outward Bound students never forget the experience. And they often find that nothing seems impossible ever again.

Outward Bound students learn to read wilderness maps.

WHAT DO YOU THINK?

What sequence of steps would you follow to build a rope bridge?

Wits Versus

by Debbie Tuseth • illustrated by Dani Jones

"I know all about this wilderness area," bragged Sam. "There are steep mountains and dangerous drop-offs. There are lots of wild animals too," he continued. "I hope we see a lynx or a bobcat. Or even a bear!"

"Well, Ranger Sam, I'm glad you're such an expert on surviving in the wilderness," Uncle Henry teased.

Sam belonged to a scouting troop. He had learned all about hiking and camping. Now he and his uncle were camping in the Colorado wilderness.

Wilderness

The sun was barely up and the grass was covered in dew. Sam and Uncle Henry started hiking. "The forecast is for clear, warm weather," said Sam. He couldn't wait to explore the unfamiliar forest.

"Look at that view!" Uncle Henry exclaimed as he pointed to mountain peaks in the distance.

Uncle Henry was a photographer (fuh-TOG-ruh-fer). He was looking forward to shooting some great photos during their expedition.

73

In the late afternoon, Sam and Uncle Henry came to a clearing near a stream. It was a perfect place to set up camp. Within a few minutes, Uncle Henry had pulled on his boots and had waded into the cool, blue water to fish. Sam stayed on shore to hunt for animal clues.

Suddenly Sam heard a sound—a whistle. It was Uncle Henry, who was pointing to the other bank.

A black bear cub was playing near the trees. "Sam!" called Uncle Henry excitedly. "Here's that wild animal you wanted to see!"

Sam knew that black bears were not usually a problem if you left them alone. But a mother bear with a cub could be very dangerous!

"Uncle Henry, get out of the water," Sam said. He tried to keep a calm voice. "The mother bear might be nearby. She will try to protect her cub."

CRASH! They heard a loud noise in the woods. A large black bear appeared behind the cub. She got on her hind legs and started to sway back and forth.

Uncle Henry waded out of the water. "Don't run, Uncle Henry," Sam said softly. "Just turn around and back away from the bear."

Together they started walking backward into the woods. But the mother bear moved toward the water.

"Wave your arms, Uncle Henry! And let's make some noise," Sam said.

Sam had learned a lot about bears in his scouting troop. He knew that if you saw one, you shouldn't run away or climb a tree. He also knew that noise could scare away a bear. And most important of all, he knew that he should stay calm. But that was hard to do. Meeting a real live bear was much different than reading about one!

"Grab some cook gear and bang it with a spoon, Uncle Henry," Sam said. They each began to bam and bang. Sam wasn't sure what was pounding louder, Uncle Henry or his heart.

At last, the bear and her cub started to move away. "Go on, go on!" Sam muttered to himself as he watched the bears leave.

"Phew! That was scary, Sam," Uncle Henry said. "But we can relax now. The bears are gone."

Later, sitting by their campfire, they relived their run-in with the bear. "I was looking for an adventure, and I really got one!" Sam said.

"That's true, Sam," Uncle Henry said. "We had an adventure. But you kept your cool too. You knew what to do and you saved the day. You could say your quick thinking came in *beary* handy."

What Do You Think?

After Sam and his uncle saw the mother bear, what steps did they take to protect themselves?

Sea Turtle Adventure

Andrea Weathers writes children's books about a place she knows well—Folly Beach, South Carolina. That's where she spent her summers as a child. And that's where she had many adventures. Here is one of them.

Ten-year-old Andie and her mom were enjoying a quiet evening at home when suddenly they heard a scream. They rushed outside to see what was wrong. But what they saw amazed them. Andie's little brother, Darrell, sat on the porch surrounded by dozens of baby sea turtles!

The turtles had just hatched from nests on the beach. But because there was no moon that night to guide them to the ocean, they had crawled toward the porch light. The baby turtles had lost their way!

Andie's mom knew just what to do. She showed Andie and Darrell how to gently scoop up the turtles and put them in buckets. Then they carried the turtles to shallow water and released them. But instead of swimming out to sea, the turtles made a U-turn and headed back toward shore! Then Andie's mom had a "bright" idea. Andie's dad could be the moon! He waded into the ocean and shined a big flashlight on the water. Now the turtles swam toward him. And this time, they stayed in the sea. Andie and her family had rescued the baby sea turtles!

ADVENTURES AND HEROES

4 for you 2 Do

Word Play

Use some of this week's vocabulary words to create a slogan for a new Outward Bound program.

adventure

wilderness

expeditions

unfamiliar

forecasts

Making Connections

What type of Outward Bound program do you think Sam might enjoy? Explain your answer.

On Paper

Which adventure from the readings would you most like to have? Write about how having this adventure might change you.

Possible Answer for Word Play: Face the unfamiliar. Have an adventure with Outward Bound!

EXTREME HOMES

Contents

EXTREME HOMES

Let's Explore

Words 2 the Wise

People live in **extreme homes** for different reasons. As you read, think about the different types of unusual homes that you have seen.

How We Live

Long ago people built houses from materials found in their environments. Some used snow blocks. Others used bamboo and palm leaves. Today, many builders are going back to using materials found in their environments. Some houses are being built from cans, logs, straw, and even garbage!

An igloo can be a shelter built from blocks of snow and ice.

Younger palm leaves are usually selected for building a hut because they are more flexible.

There is no shortage of palm trees on tropical islands. So why not build a house out of them? Palm huts are made from palm leaves.

Palm huts are lightweight and waterproof. At the same time they are cool because they allow air to move in and out. The roofs on many palm huts will only last a few years.

Would you live in a house built from what others throw away? In the 1970s, some people started building houses made from recycled materials. Walls are made of old tires filled with dirt. Renewable resources power these houses. The sun is used for heat and electricity. People living in these houses don't use very much water.

Energy is becoming more and more expensive. Many people think that recycled materials are a good solution to this problem.

In many places, people are building houses made of straw. Straw bale houses are tough. The thick bales are packed tightly. These houses are warm in winter and cool in summer. The walls are covered in stucco. Stucco is a type of cement that is put on the outside walls. When finished they look just like any other house.

Look around your neighborhood. What kinds of materials could you use to build a house?

Straw bale homes are practically soundproof.

LIVING DOWN UNDER

BY PATRICIA MCFADDEN

Australia is called "the land down under." But for the people of Coober Pedy, this means way down under. They live underground!

In Coober Pedy, Australia, temperatures can reach 120 degrees. That's hot! There is not much water. There are few trees. This means there are not a lot of materials to use to build houses. That leaves only one place to go—underground.

Coober Pedy, Australia, lies in the middle of the Australian desert.

AUSTRALIA

COOBER PEDY

THE COOLEST PLACE TO ESCAPE THE HEAT

The native Australians thought it was funny to see people living underground. They called it *kupa piti* (KOO-puh PIT-tee). This means "white man's hole."

Miles and miles of red treeless desert surround the town of Coober Pedy. On the surface, there are some buildings and cars. It doesn't look like much of a town.

But there are stores, churches, hotels, and houses. They are all underground. It is the coolest place to escape the heat.

From above ground the town of Coober Pedy doesn't look very exciting.

EXTREME HOMES

Raised hills of dirt signal an entry to an underground world.

While in Coober Pedy you can spend the night in an underground hotel. There the temperatures stay at about 60 degrees Fahrenheit all year long. It is cool and comfortable.

There is so much going on under the surface. In this town many people shop, eat, and sleep underground. But why do people want to live in these extreme houses? And what is it that brings people from all over the world to this underground town?

Many visitors say they like sleeping underground.

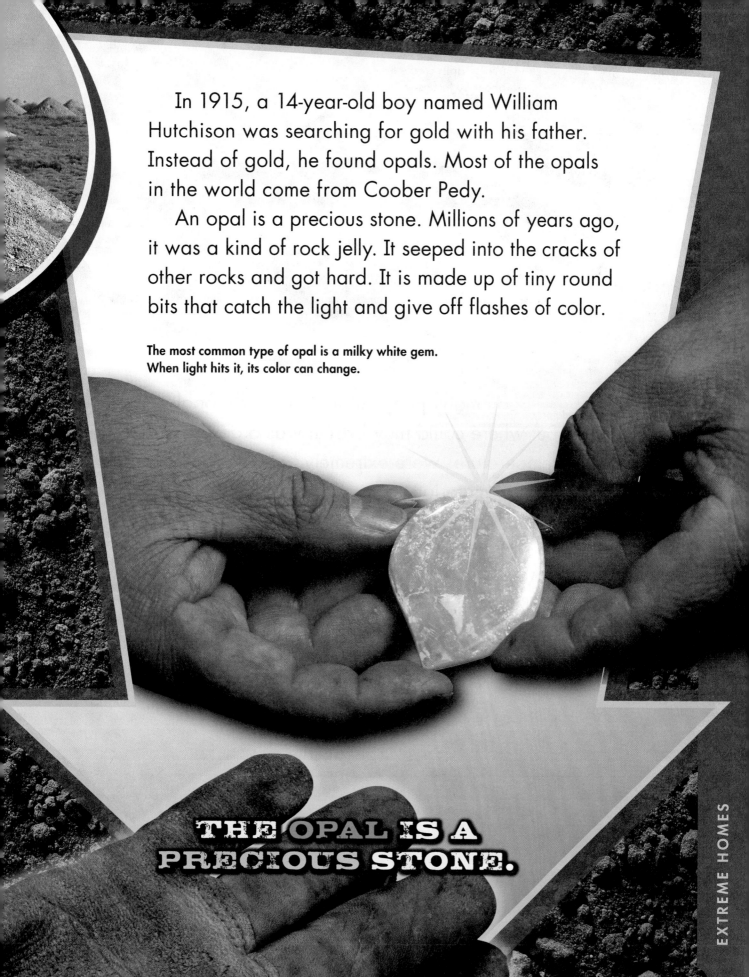

In 1915, a 14-year-old boy named William Hutchison was searching for gold with his father. Instead of gold, he found opals. Most of the opals in the world come from Coober Pedy.

An opal is a precious stone. Millions of years ago, it was a kind of rock jelly. It seeped into the cracks of other rocks and got hard. It is made up of tiny round bits that catch the light and give off flashes of color.

The most common type of opal is a milky white gem. When light hits it, its color can change.

THE OPAL IS A PRECIOUS STONE.

Mining drills create holes about 40 inches wide and can dig up to 100 feet deep.

Soon many people came to dig for opals. But where could they live? It was a desert. The temperatures were extremely hot. There were not a lot of materials to use to build shelters. They had to find a cool place to live.

Many of the opal hunters had been soldiers in World War I. On the battlefields they lived in underground shelters called trenches. The opal mines reminded the soldiers of the trenches. They decided to use them for homes.

During World War I, soldiers lived in trenches like these.

People found that the underground homes were cool in the summer and warm in the winter. Soon people began making more underground houses. Today, Coober Pedy is famous for its underground architecture. About 3,500 people live in Coober Pedy. More than half of them live underground.

Building a house in Coober Pedy really means "digging a house." People use a shovel or a drilling machine. They are like giant gophers drilling to build a house.

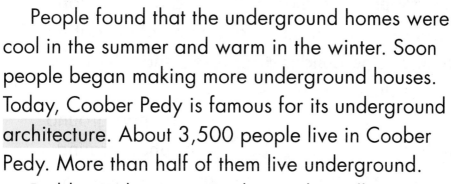

UNDERGROUND HOUSES DON'T NEED TO BE PAINTED!

In Coober Pedy, digging to build a house can be exciting. You can also make some money at the same time. One builder discovered enough opals to pay for the entire house.

A drilling machine can dig out an underground space in a single day. A burrow, or underground hole, is a simple home. It does not have the outside architecture of typical houses. But it is much less expensive than houses built above the ground.

An underground home has no need for wood or bricks. The roof and walls are made from the earth.

CAVE-LIKE HOUSES GAVE FILMMAKERS EXTREME SCENERY.

Coober Pedy has been used many times as a movie set. The treeless red desert and cave-like houses gave filmmakers the extreme scenery they were looking for.

But for visitors and residents of Coober Pedy it is the shiny cool gems that they are looking for. The burrows offer protection from the heat and dust. And the stories of great opal discoveries fill them with a secret hope of one day striking it rich!

WHAT DO YOU THINK?

Why do the people of Coober Pedy live underground?

A Sea of GRASS

by Michael Archer

AN AMERICAN DREAM

In 1862, the news spread quickly. The government was giving away land in the middle of the United States. All you had to do was pay a fee and live on the land for five years. After that, it belonged to you.

In those days, many people didn't own land. They thought this was the perfect opportunity. Owning land was the American dream!

NOTHING BUT GRASS

People packed up everything they owned and moved west. They didn't know what to expect. They traveled by train, covered wagon, and even on foot. They moved to places like Kansas, North Dakota, Oklahoma, and Nebraska.

When they arrived they noticed that there were very few trees. They found a sea of grass. It stretched as far as the eye could see. It was called a prairie. The people who would build their homes on these prairies were called homesteaders.

Many men moved west alone. Later they sent for their families.

Sod houses were sturdy and easy to build.

SOD BUSTERS

The homesteaders quickly adapted to life on the prairie. There weren't many trees or stones to use for building houses. They had to use what was available to them. They noticed that the grass, or sod, was like a thick mat. It was difficult to plow through.

So someone decided to build a house out of this sod. They cut it into pieces. Then they stacked the pieces like bricks. They left spaces for windows and doors.

Homesteaders who built their houses out of sod were called "sod busters." Their houses were called "soddies." Soon soddies were being built all across the Great Plains. The soddies were good shelters for life on the prairie.

"Dugouts" were soddies that were built into the side of a hill. The roofs were made of cedar poles and strips of sod. Because there weren't many trees, cedar poles had to be brought from far away. Sod strips were laid across the poles.

An entire family lived in this dugout in Oklahoma.

LIFE ON THE PRAIRIE

Life on the prairie was difficult for the homesteaders. They had to adapt to harsh weather. Winters were very cold. Summers were very hot. They faced blizzards, tornados, and dust storms. And the wind was always blowing. If a fire started, the strong winds would spread it quickly across the fields.

Winters on the prairie were long and cold.

The Haumont family built this two-story sod house in Nebraska. Inside a sod house it was often dark and damp.

Homesteaders also worried about water. It was in short supply. Barrels of water were hauled in from miles away. Some homesteaders had to dig wells by hand.

Life inside the soddies was not much better. Soddies were damp and dark. They smelled like dirt. And because they were part dirt, soddies had problems with mice, snakes, and bugs coming through the walls. If it rained, the floors would turn to thick mud. It was hard to keep soddies clean.

WHY DID THEY DO IT?

Life on the prairie wasn't easy. The climate was harsh. There was little medical care. The houses were dirty. So why would anyone choose to face such hardships?

Homesteaders wanted their own land. For them it was a dream that was worth the struggle. It was this dream that kept them going. If they could stay there long enough, the land would be theirs. But five years is a long time.

Many tourists visit this sod house in Nebraska.

Only about half of the people who tried to homestead stayed. Many went back East to bigger cities.

One homesteader named Mattie left a record of photographs and letters of her life on the prairie. Her words painted a picture of life in a sod house. She wrote on June 16, 1873:

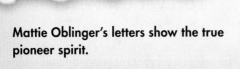

I expect you think we live miserable because we are in a sod house, but I tell you in solid earnest I never enjoyed myself better.

Mattie Oblinger's letters show the true pioneer spirit.

WHAT DO YOU THINK?

Why was a house made of sod a good choice for the homesteaders?

OLD LOG HOUSE

by James S. Tippett

On a little green knoll
At the edge of the wood
My great great grandmother's
First house stood.

The house was of logs
My grandmother said
With one big room
And a lean-to shed.

The logs were cut
And the house was raised
By pioneer men
In the olden days.

I like to hear
My grandmother tell
How they built the fireplace
And dug the well.

They split the shingles;
They filled each chink;
It's a house of which
I like to think.

Forever and ever
I wish I could
Live in a house
At the edge of a wood.

Houses

by Aileen Fisher

House are faces
(haven't you found?)
with their hats in the air,
and their necks in the ground.

Windows are noses,
windows are eyes,
and doors are the mouths
of a suitable size.

And a porch—or the place
where porches begin—
is just like a mustache
shading the chin.

4 YOU 2 DO

Word Play

Change the word **adapt** to fit each sentence.
Use the endings –ed, –ing, or –ation.

Homesteaders adapt____ to life on the prairie.

Adapt____ to life on the prairie wasn't easy.

The miners in Australia made a good
adapt____ to life in the desert.

Change the endings of other vocabulary
words from this week and write your
own sentences.

Making Connections

How are the houses in Coober
Pedy like soddies?

On Paper

Where would you like to live,
in Coober Pedy or in a soddy?

Answers for Word Play: adapted, adapting, adaptation

Contents

THE MOON

Words 2 the Wise

The moon has fascinated people for centuries. As you read, think about why people might have created stories and myths about the moon. How are they different from what you know about the moon?

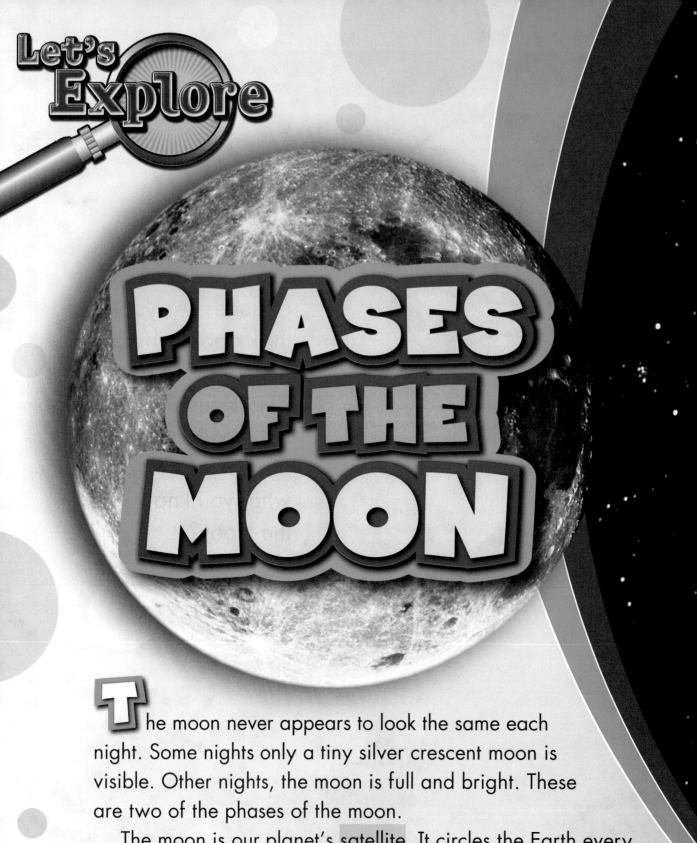

PHASES OF THE MOON

The moon never appears to look the same each night. Some nights only a tiny silver crescent moon is visible. Other nights, the moon is full and bright. These are two of the phases of the moon.

The moon is our planet's satellite. It circles the Earth every 29 days. The sun's light hits the moon at different angles as it revolves around the Earth. This light creates the phases of the moon.

NEW MOON

A new moon is dark. This means the side we can see is not being lit by the sun.

FIRST QUARTER

Now the moon is a quarter of the way around the Earth.

FULL MOON

The full moon is halfway around the Earth. The side we can see is lit by the sun.

LAST QUARTER

Now the moon is three-quarters of the way around the Earth.

From Earth, the moon seems to grow or fade away. We call this waxing and waning. A waxing moon appears to be growing larger. A waning moon appears to be getting smaller.

One Moon, Many Myths

by Martin Houlihan

illustrated by Joel Nakamura

Look at a clear night sky. What do you see?
You see stars and planets and perhaps an airplane.
What else? You see the moon, of course. You see
the moon waxing or waning* in the sky. Everyone
on Earth sees the same object revolving around
the Earth. We call the moon our satellite. But does
everyone on Earth see the same moon?

*A waxing moon grows larger until it's full. A waning moon grows smaller until
there's no moon.

People have always told stories about the moon. Some of these stories are myths. They try to explain why the moon changes its shape. Or they tell what people see when they look at the moon.

From Earth, people can see shadowy spots on the moon. These spots look like faces, animals, and other things in the light and shadows. Everyone sees something different. Have you ever seen things while looking at the moon?

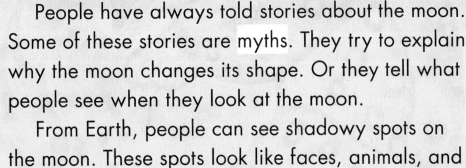

In the 1600s, an astronomer first looked at the moon using a telescope. He thought there were seas on the moon.

Jaguars and Brushfires

Stories about the moon tell us a lot about the people who tell them. For example, one myth from South America tells about a jaguar living on the moon. Jaguars are native to South America. Other places might use other animals in their stories.

American cowboys told one myth about someone starting a brushfire on the moon. Cowboys saw a lot of brushfires on the prairie.

Cloud Maker

Native Hawaiians have a myth about a beautiful moon maiden named Hina (HEE-na). One night Hina crossed a rainbow bridge to the moon. She became the maker of clouds. Hina would sit on the moon and beat the bark of a tree into a soft cloth. Then, she would throw the cloth over the Earth, and it would become clouds.

The beating of bark is something that Hawaiians do. This myth explains something that Hawaiians understand.

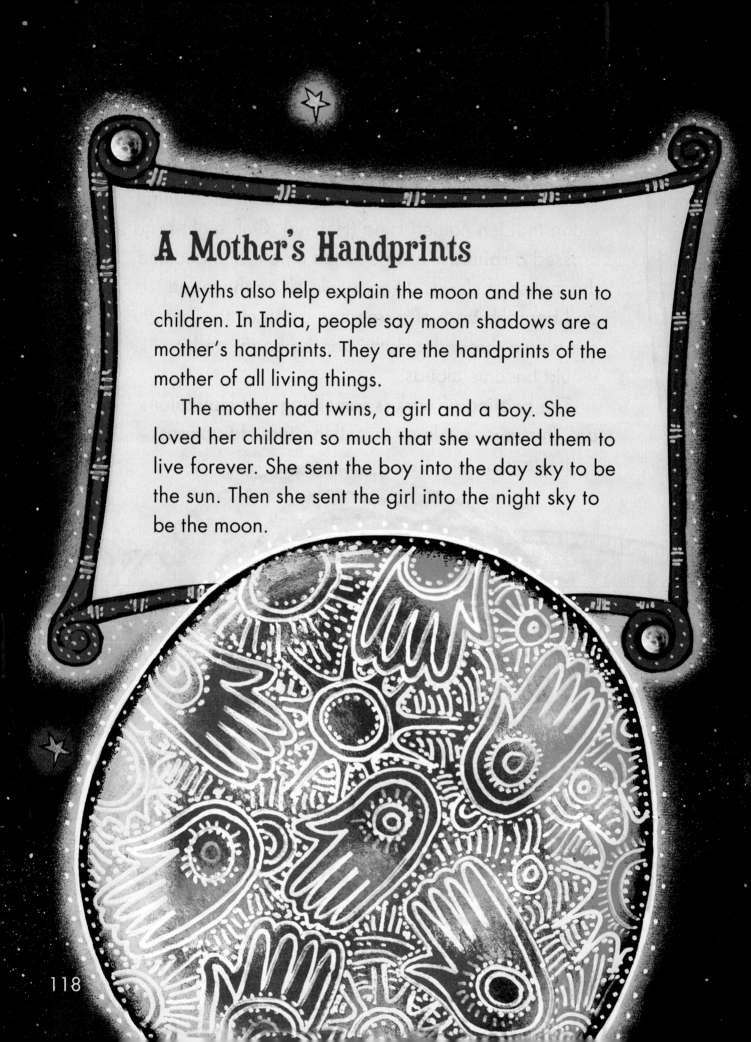

A Mother's Handprints

Myths also help explain the moon and the sun to children. In India, people say moon shadows are a mother's handprints. They are the handprints of the mother of all living things.

The mother had twins, a girl and a boy. She loved her children so much that she wanted them to live forever. She sent the boy into the day sky to be the sun. Then she sent the girl into the night sky to be the moon.

Shy Baloo

Native Australians say that the moon is the face of a man named Baloo (BA-loo). One day Baloo fell into the water in front of some girls. The girls laughed.

Baloo ran back to the night sky to hide in embarrassment. After a few days, his courage returned. He showed more and more of his face. Soon his whole face could be seen again. But every month, Baloo remembers his embarrassment and ducks back out of sight.

What is the truth about the moon?

Moon myths try to explain many things about the moon. But what do we *really* know about it?

We know that the moon is Earth's satellite. That means it orbits around the Earth. We know that the moon isn't really round like a ball. It is almost shaped like an egg. How did we find out these things? Astronomers!

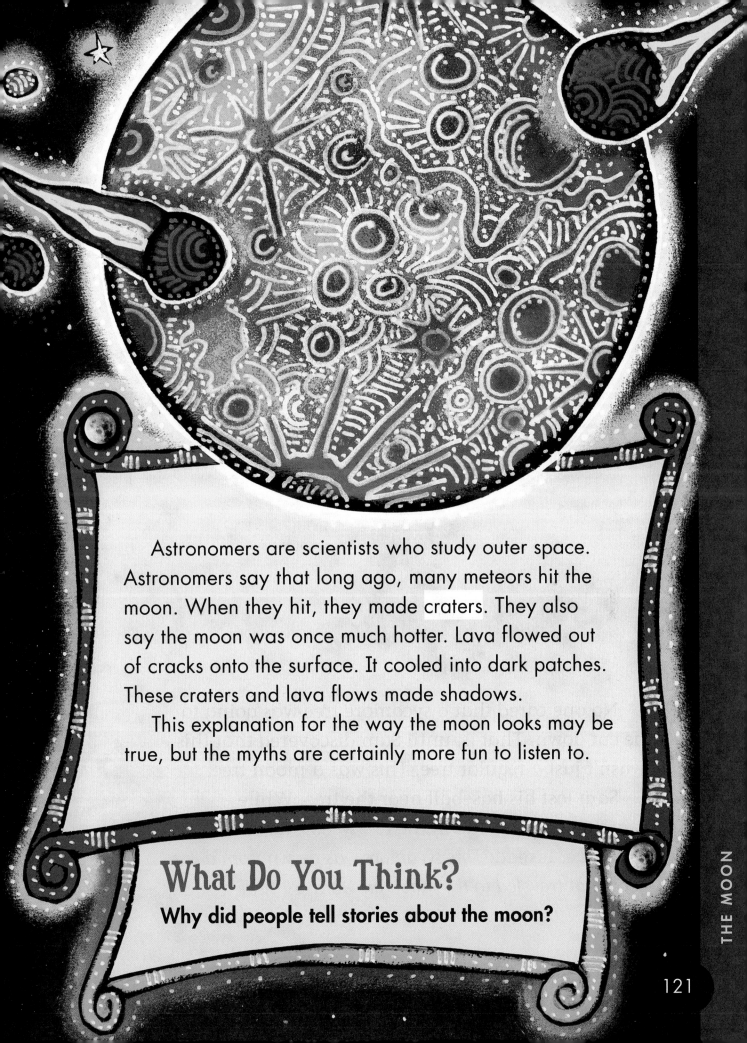

Astronomers are scientists who study outer space. Astronomers say that long ago, many meteors hit the moon. When they hit, they made craters. They also say the moon was once much hotter. Lava flowed out of cracks onto the surface. It cooled into dark patches. These craters and lava flows made shadows.

This explanation for the way the moon looks may be true, but the myths are certainly more fun to listen to.

What Do You Think?

Why did people tell stories about the moon?

Saving the Moon Tree

by Kayla Meginnis
illustrated by Lee White

No one cared that a sycamore tree was going to be cut down. That is, until Sam discovered that this wasn't just a regular tree. This was a moon tree.

Sam lost his baseball near the tree. While searching for the ball in the tall weeds, he uncovered a plaque. It read: *This sycamore was grown from a seed that traveled to the moon on* Apollo 14, *in January 1971.*

Sticks with red flags surrounded the vacant lot. Soon bulldozers would clear the weeds and the tree to make room for a new convenience store.

Sam had never heard of a moon tree. He and his friend, Rick, went to their teacher, Ms. Johnson. She knew a lot about astronomy.

"A moon tree!" she exclaimed. "Here in our town?" Ms. Johnson had some information on moon trees. The boys decided to do some more research at the library.

Sam found a book on the *Apollo 14* space mission. Rick searched on the Internet.

Sam read that an astronaut named Stuart Roosa brought tree seeds with him on the *Apollo 14* space mission. Roosa liked trees. Before he was an astronaut, he was a smokejumper.

The seeds circled the moon 34 times. People didn't know if the trees would grow. But they did grow. They became known as moon trees.

"Look at this!" exclaimed Rick. "They planted over 400 moon trees!"

Fig. 1 - APOLLO

Over time, most people forgot about the moon trees. But a man named Dave Williams was making a map of where all the trees were planted. He knew how important this was.

They asked Ms. Johnson what they should do. "I'm sure most people in town don't remember the moon seeds," said Ms. Johnson. "You need to let people know that this tree was part of space exploration."

Sam grinned. "I have an idea," he said.

Sam wrote an article and sent it to the town newspaper. Rick wrote a petition. The petition asked the mayor to help save the moon tree. He and several other students waited outside the grocery store asking people to sign the petition.

As people left the store, the boys would tell them about the *Apollo 14* space mission and the moon trees. People were very interested. Soon they had 128 signatures on the petition.

When the moon tree article was published,
the newspaper office got dozens of calls. Everyone
wanted to help Sam.

Mr. Hardy, the owner of the vacant lot, read the
article too. He called Sam's mom. He said that he
wanted to meet Sam.

"What does he want?" Sam nervously asked.

"He didn't say," his mom said. "But don't worry."

The next day, Sam and Rick were sitting on his
porch when a car pulled up in front of his house.

"Are you Sam?" a man asked as he approached the boys. "My name is Mr. Hardy. I wanted to meet you in person and thank you for your important discovery. I bought that land eight years ago. No one ever told me about the moon tree."

"Does that mean that you won't build your store?" Sam asked hopefully.

"Oh, I'm still going to build my store," Mr. Hardy said. "But I have an idea."

Six months later, the store was built. Next to the store was the sycamore tree. Around the tree was a grassy area with a picnic table.

On the day of the grand opening, everyone gathered around the new Apollo Convenience Store. Mr. Hardy had bought a new plaque for the moon tree. The plaque had the same statement as before, but Mr. Hardy also added these words: *This moon tree is dedicated to Sam Weller and Rick Garcia.*

What Do You Think?

Why were Sam and Rick able to save the moon tree?

MOON FACTS

Sometimes the moon is totally hidden from our view in the night sky. It may last up to two hours. This is called an eclipse (ee-CLIPS).

Long ago, people explained this phenomenon by saying that a dragon had eaten the moon. Today, we know this is not true. Astronomers know why eclipses happen and can predict when the next one will occur.

Did You Know? The moon reflects light from our sun. The color of the moon when we see it depends on how much pollution or smoke is in our air.

Did You Know? An eclipse will occur in North and South America on April 15, 2014; October 8, 2014; April 4, 2015; and September 27, 2015.

The sun is much bigger than the Earth. When it shines on our planet, we cast a shadow into outer space. Sometimes, as the moon revolves around the Earth, it lines up perfectly with the sun and Earth. This causes Earth to cast a total shadow on the moon. This is an eclipse!

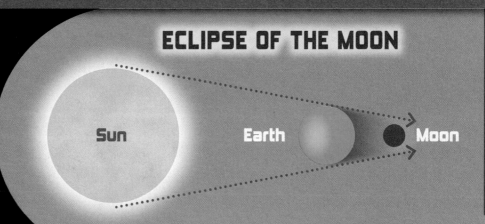

ECLIPSE OF THE MOON

Sun   Earth   Moon

PLANTING BY MOON PHASES

Some gardeners watch the moon very closely. They believe that you should plant leaf crops, such as lettuce, when the moon is waxing. They think you should plant root crops, such as potatoes, when the moon is waning.

Did You Know? The moon is moving away from Earth. Long ago, the moon looked three times larger than it does today.

Did You Know? The moon circles the Earth at over 2,000 miles per hour.

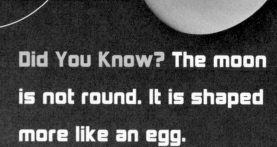

Did You Know? The moon is not round. It is shaped more like an egg.

Did You Know? There have been 12 people who have walked on the surface of the moon.

Did You Know?

The moon is not made of cheese.

4 YOU 2 DO

Word Play

See if you can answer these space jokes.
Then see if you can come up with your own
space jokes using this week's vocabulary words.

1. How is the moon like a dollar?
2. Where do astronauts leave their spaceships?
3. Why couldn't the astronaut buy a ticket
   to the moon?

Making Connections

Why do you think the moon is interesting
to astronomers and storytellers?

On Paper

People have many myths about the phases
of the moon. In two or three sentences,
come up with your own explanation for
why the moon changes.

Answers for Word Play: 1. They both have four quarters.
2. At the parking meteors. 3. It was full.

Glossary

a·dapt (ə dapt′), *VERB*. 1. to change something to fit different conditions; adjust: *They adapted the barn for use as a studio.* 2. to change yourself; get used to something: *He adapted to the new school with no problem.* **a·dapt·ed, a·dapt·ing.**

ad·ven·ture (ad ven′ chər), *NOUN*. an unusual or exciting experience: *Her trip to Alaska was quite an adventure.*

an·cient (ān′ shənt), *ADJECTIVE*. belonging to times long past: *The ancient city of Bam, in Iran, is more than 2,000 years old.*

ar·chi·tec·ture (är′ kə tek′ chər), *NOUN*. 1. the science and art of designing buildings: *Robert studied architecture in Europe.* 2. a style or special manner of building: *Columns are used in Greek architecture.*

ar·ti·fact (är′ tə fakt), *NOUN.* anything made by human skill or work, especially a tool: *Museums have gold coins and other artifacts from ancient times.* PL. **ar·ti·facts.**

as·tro·naut (as′ trə nôt), *NOUN.* a person who has been trained to fly in a spacecraft: *While in space, astronauts repair space stations and do experiments.*

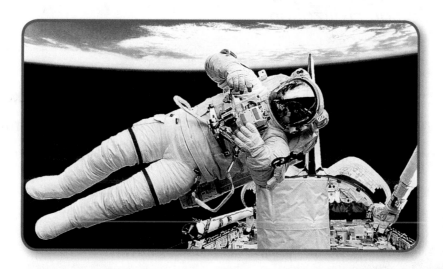

as·tron·o·mer (ə stron′ ə mər), *NOUN.* someone who is an expert in studying the sun, moon, planets, stars, and other objects in space: *The astronomer observed the rings of Saturn through the telescope.* PL. **as·tron·o·mers.**

a in hat	ō in open	sh in she
ā in age	ȯ in all	th in thin
â in care	ô in order	ŦH in then
ä in far	oi in oil	zh in measure
e in let	ou in out	ə = a in about
ē in equal	u in cup	ə = e in taken
ėr in term	u̇ in put	ə = i in pencil
i in it	ü in rule	ə = o in lemon
ī in ice	ch in child	ə = u in circus
o in hot	ng in long	

bur·row (bėr′ ō), NOUN. a hole dug in the ground by a person or an animal for shelter or protection: *Rabbits live in burrows.*

civ·i·li·za·tion (siv′ ə lə zā′ shən), NOUN. a group of people who work together in many ways, such as building cities, making laws, and creating art: *Many of our laws are from ancient Roman civilization.*

cra·ter (krā′ tər), NOUN. 1. a hole in the ground shaped like a bowl: *This crater was made by a meteorite.* 2. the opening at the top of a volcano: *Lava flowed from the volcano's crater.* PL. **cra·ters.**

dan·ger·ous (dān′ jər əs), ADJECTIVE. not safe; likely to harm you: *Fireworks can be dangerous.*

de·stroy (di stroi/), *VERB.* to damage something very badly; ruin: *A tornado destroyed the house.* **de·stroyed, de·stroy·ing.**

ex·cit·ing (ek sī/ ting), *ADJECTIVE.* causing strong lively feelings; thrilling: *We read an exciting story about pirates and buried treasure.*

ex·pe·di·tion (ek/ spə dish/ ən), *NOUN.* 1. a long, well-planned trip for a special purpose, such as exploration or scientific study: *The astronauts went on an expedition to the moon.* 2. the people, ships, and so on, that make such a trip: *The expedition searched for the lost gold.* *PL.* **ex·pe·di·tions.**

ex·treme (ek strēm/), *ADJECTIVE.* much more than usual; very great: *The extreme heat caused people to stay inside.*

a in hat	ō in open	sh in she
ā in age	ȯ in all	th in thin
â in care	ô in order	̱TH in then
ä in far	oi in oil	zh in measure
e in let	ou in out	ə = a in about
ē in equal	u in cup	ə = e in taken
ėr in term	u̇ in put	ə = i in pencil
i in it	ü in rule	ə = o in lemon
ī in ice	ch in child	ə = u in circus
o in hot	ng in long	

fore·cast (fôr′ kast′), NOUN. a statement of what is going to happen: *The weather forecast calls for cloudy skies and light rain.* PL. **fore·casts.**

haz·ard (haz′ ərd), NOUN. something that may cause damage or injury: *Icy roads are a hazard for drivers.* PL. **haz·ards.**

her·o (hir′ ō), NOUN. someone admired for his or her bravery, great deeds, or noble qualities: *The firefighter who rescued the dog from a burning building was a hero.* PL. **her·oes.**

home·stead·er (hōm′ sted′ ər), NOUN. a person who builds a house on the prairie: *After they traveled west by wagon, many homesteaders built their homes on the prairie.* PL. **home·stead·ers.**

mis·sion (mish′ ən), NOUN. a task that people are sent somewhere to do: *The astronaut was sent on a mission to the moon.*

myth (mith), NOUN. a legend or story, usually one that attempts to explain something in nature: *There are several myths about why the moon changes shape.* PL. **myths.**

prair·ie (prâr′ ē), NOUN. a large area of level or rolling land with grass but few or no trees: *Buffalo roamed the prairie.* PL. **prair·ies.**

pro·fes·sion (prə fesh′ ən), NOUN. an occupation, such as law, medicine, or teaching, that requires special training and study: *She chose teaching as her profession.*

a in hat	ō in open	sh in she
ā in age	ȯ in all	th in thin
â in care	ô in order	ŦH in then
ä in far	oi in oil	zh in measure
e in let	ou in out	ə = a in about
ē in equal	u in cup	ə = e in taken
ėr in term	u̇ in put	ə = i in pencil
i in it	ü in rule	ə = o in lemon
ī in ice	ch in child	ə = u in circus
o in hot	ng in long	

sat·el·lite (sat′ l īt), NOUN. an astronomical object that revolves around a planet; a moon: *The moon is a satellite of Earth.*

so·ci·e·ty (sə sī′ ə tē), NOUN. 1. all the people; human beings living together as a group: *Society must work hard for world peace.* 2. a group of people joined together for a common purpose or by common interests: *Mark and Tim belong to the same society for people interested in science.*

stat·ue (stach′ ü), NOUN. a figure made from stone, wood or metal to look like a person or animal: *The statue of Lincoln is visited by millions of people every year.* PL. **stat·ues.**

the·a·ter or **the·a·tre** (thē′ ə tər), NOUN. a place where people go to see movies, plays, or performances: *We went to the theater in the city to see a play.*

tra·di·tion (trə dish′ ən), *NOUN.* the process of handing down beliefs, opinions, customs, and stories from parents to children: *One tradition in my family is a picnic on the Fourth of July.* PL. **tra·di·tions.**

un·fa·mil·iar (un′ fə mil′ yər), *ADJECTIVE.* not well-known; unusual; strange: *That handwriting is unfamiliar to me.*

wil·der·ness (wil′ dər nis), *NOUN.* a wild place; region with few or no people living in it: *They nearly got lost in the wilderness.* PL. **wil·der·ness·es.**

a in hat	ō in open	sh in she
ā in age	ȯ in all	th in thin
â in care	ô in order	ŦH in then
ä in far	oi in oil	zh in measure
e in let	ou in out	ə = a in about
ē in equal	u in cup	ə = e in taken
ėr in term	ù in put	ə = i in pencil
i in it	ü in rule	ə = o in lemon
ī in ice	ch in child	ə = u in circus
o in hot	ng in long	

Acknowledgments

Text

Every effort has been made to locate the copyright owner of material reproduced in this component. Omissions brought to our attention will be corrected in subsequent editions. Grateful acknowledgment is made to the following for copyrighted material.

106 HarperCollins "Old Log House" by James Tippett from *A World to Know*. Copyright © 1933 by Harper & Row. Renewed © 1961 by Martha Tippett. Used by permission of HarperCollins Publishers.

107 Marian Reiner, Literary Agent "Houses" by Aileen Fisher from *Up the Windy Hill*. Copyright © 1953, 1981 by Aileen Fisher. Used by permission of Marian Reiner on behalf of the Boulder Public Library Foundation, Inc.

Illustrations

20–26, Cover Neil Shigley; **41** Don Burmeister; **46–52** Chris Lensch; **72–79** Dani Jones; **106** Franklin Hammond; **115–119, Cover** Joel Nakamura; **122–128** Lee White.

Photographs

Every effort has been made to secure permission and provide appropriate credit for photographic material. The publisher deeply regrets any omission and pledges to correct errors called to its attention in subsequent editions.

Unless otherwise acknowledged, all photographs are the property of Pearson Education, Inc.

Photo locators denoted as follows: Top (T), Center (C), Bottom (B), Left (L), Right (R), Background (Bkgd)

Cover (TR, BR, Back) Getty Images, (TL) Harry Taylor/©DK Images, (CL) Ingram Publishing 1 (CL) Ingram Publishing; **2** (CR) ©Corbis/SuperStock, (B) ©Richard A. Cooke/Corbis, (B) nagelestock/Alamy Images; **3** (TR, BR) Getty Images, (CR) Robert Harding Picture Library Ltd/Alamy Images; **5** (C) PhotoLibrary Group, Inc.; **6** (TR) ©Barbara Stitzer/PhotoEdit, Inc., (CR) ©Reuben Schulz/©iStockphoto; **7** (CR) ©Corbis/SuperStock, (CL) Getty Images; **8** (C) ©Barbara Stitzer/PhotoEdit, Inc.; **9** (TR) ©Corbis/SuperStock, (BC) ©Spencer Grant/PhotoEdit, Inc.; **11** (CR) ©Jeff Greenberg/Alamy Images; **12** (T) ©George Doyle/Getty Images; **13** (C) Getty Images; **14** (B) Vince Streano/Getty Images; **15** (CR) ©Gabriela Hasbun/Getty Images; **16** (C) ©Tony Freeman/PhotoEdit, Inc., (CR) ©bst2012/Fotolia; **17** (TR) ©Glowimages/Getty Images, (CR) ©Reuben Schulz/©iStockphoto; **18** (C) ©Kayte M. Deioma/PhotoEdit, Inc.; **19** (T) ©Seth Wenig/Star Ledger/Corbis, (B) ©Thomas Northcut/Getty Images; **28** (T) ©A.T. Willett/Alamy Images, (B) ©Visions of America LLC/Alamy Images, (CL) Bruce Chambers/Corbis, (TL) NASA Goddard Space Flight Center/NASA Image Exchange; **30** (CR) Getty Images; **31** (C) Pete Turner/Getty Images; **32** (BR) ©Imagestate Media Partners Limited - Impact Photos/Alamy Images, (TCR) nagelestock/Alamy Images; **33** (CL) ©Richard A. Cooke/Corbis, (CL) Archaeological Museum Istanbul/Dagli Orti/The Art Archive, (CC) Bridgeman Art Library, (BR) Robert Harding/Getty Images; **34** (C) nagelestock/Alamy Images; **35** (T) Ray Juno/Corbis, (B) Wilmar Photography/Alamy Images; **36** (T) nagelestock/Alamy Images; **37** (B) Andre Jenny/Alamy Images, (T) Stock Montage, Inc./Alamy Images; **38** (C) ©Richard A. Cooke/Corbis, (BL) Getty Images; **39** (B) Getty Images; **40** (T) Michael S. Lewis/Corbis; **41** (BR) Getty Images; **42** (T) Richard A. Cooke/Corbis; **44** (TR) Getty Images, (TL, C) Richard A. Cooke/Corbis; **46** (CR) Getty Images; **47** (C) MedioImages/Getty Images; **48** (TL) Archaeological Museum Istanbul/Dagli Orti/The Art Archive, (TR) Bridgeman Art Library; **53** (BR) Bridgeman Art Library; **54** (L) Getty Images, (R) Mimmo Jodice/Corbis; **55** (TR) ©Imagestate Media Partners Limited - Impact Photos/Alamy Images; **56** (BR) Robert Harding/Getty Images; **57** (C) ©Neville Dawson/PhotoLibrary Group, Inc.; **58** (BC) ©Morales Morales/PhotoLibrary Group, Inc., (CR) David Levenson/Alamy Images; **59** (T) Getty Images, (BL) John and Lisa Merrill/Corbis; **60** (T) Getty Images; **61** (T) ©Ryan McGinnis/Alamy; **62** (B) Getty Images; **63** (C) Mediscan/Alamy Images; **80** (B) ©Aqua Image/Alamy Images, (B) ©Reinhard Dirscherl/PhotoLibrary Group, Inc., (CR) Courtesy of Andrea Weathers; **81** (T) ©Morales Morales/PhotoLibrary Group, Inc., (TR) ©STILLFX/Shutterstock; **82** (CR) John and Lisa Merrill/Corbis; **83** (C) Robert Harding Picture Library Ltd/Alamy Images; **84** (C) Harry Taylor/©DK Images, (TCR) Johner Images/Getty Images, (BC) Library of Congress; **85** (TL) R. Ian Lloyd/Masterfile Corporation, (CL) Solomon D. Butcher/Library of Congress; **86** (C) Johner Images/Getty Images; **87** (C) Joanna McCarthy/Getty Images, (TR) Willard R Culver/Getty Images; **88** (BR) Getty Images, (C) Roger Bamber/Alamy Images; **89** (T, BL) ©Michelle Mahood; **90** (T) Getty Images, (CL) Harry Taylor/©DK Images; **91** (TC) Alessandro Gandolfi/Index Stock Imagery, (B) Paul A. Souders/Corbis; **92** (Bkgd, BCL) Getty Images, (TR) Paul A. Souders/Corbis, (BC) Ralph Krubner/Index Stock Imagery; **93** (BL) Getty Images, (CC) Paul A. Souders/Corbis; **94** (Bkgd) Getty Images, (T) Paul A. Souders/Corbis, (BL) The Granger Collection, NY; **95** (R) Getty Images, (BL) R. Ian Lloyd/Masterfile Corporation; **96** (Bkgd) Getty Images, (B) Paul A. Souders/Corbis; **97** (T) Alessandro Gandolfi/Index Stock Imagery, (B) Getty Images; **98** (T) ©Lars Johansson/Fotolia; **99** (BC) James L. Amos/Corbis; **100** (Bkgrd) ©William Manning/Alamy Images, (TL) Joseph H. Young/Library of Congress, (CR) Solomon D. Butcher/Library of Congress; **101** (BC) ©Dedrick/Library of Congress; **102** (BL) Daryl Benso/Masterfile Corporation, (C) Getty Images; **103** (TL) Philip Gould/Corbis, (TR) Solomon D. Butcher/Library of Congress; **104** (Bkgrd) ©John Glover/Alamy Images, (BC) ©Tom Till/Alamy Images; **105** (CR) Library of Congress; **108** (BR) Steve Nichols/Alamy Images; **109** (B) Frank Chmura/Getty Images, (TC) Jupiter Images; **110** (TR, BC) Getty Images; **111** (BR, BL) Getty Images, (C) Paramount Television/The Kobal Collection; **112** Getty Images; **113** (C) John Sanford/Photo Researchers, Inc.; **114** (T) Peter Arnold, Inc/Alamy Images; **115** (B) Getty Images; **120** (B) Getty Images; **130** (B) Jeff Vanuga/Corbis; **132** (B) ©Royalty-Free/Corbis; **133** (TR, CL, BR) Getty Images; **134** (BR) Brand X Pictures; **136** (CR) Wilmar Photography/Alamy Images; **137** (B) Getty Images; **138** (B) Getty Images; **139** (TR) Digital Stock; **140** (B) James L. Amos/Corbis; **141** (CR) ©Keith Levit Photography/Index Open; **143** (CR) ©AbleStock/Index Open.